YOUR
BUDGET

The Essential Guide to Financial Health

Recommended for Adults and Teens

Why I wrote this guide

Plenty has been written and published about the subject of budgeting. So why did I decide to write this guide? Two reasons. The first stems from my work experiences. The second comes from my abiding faith in people's ability to seek and follow the road to financial health.

While practicing bankruptcy and foreclosure law in the state of Florida, I saw too many people get caught in downward financial spirals that resulted in the loss of personal confidence, broken dreams, and even divorce. As painful as this was to witness, I was able to get an inside view on how these folks viewed their finances, and how they arrived at the decisions they did. With that knowledge at hand, I felt that a new guide would help others who might be headed toward financial distress, or who just wanted to get a better handle on their finances.

My experiences helping to develop and manage budgets at an energy company and hospital also influenced my decision to write this guide. While engaged in budget planning, I realized that the principles relied upon in large organizations were really no different than what individuals would use to budget for themselves, albeit on a smaller scale. It is my intent to share these principles with you.

The other reason for writing this guide is more global in scope. Each of us contributes in a small way to the overall economic health and progress of our nation. When we make choices that allow us to fulfill (or even come close to fulfilling) our financial potential, the combined benefit can be enormous. This in turn leads to better financial opportunities, better job growth and less financial risk for all. Therefore, it is my hope that by employing the methods presented, readers will take steps that have a positive impact on the community at large.

I would like to thank Morgan Pecman for her editing help and suggestions.

Robert F. "Fritz" VanVolkenburgh

Chapter 1: Introduction to Budgeting

The power of effective budgeting cannot be overestimated. Budgeting provides a clear picture of our finances, and serves as a personalized blueprint for future spending. Without it we're like a sailor without a compass on a starless night. The good news is that anybody can budget. If your math skills are fuzzy, or you don't have a ton of free time on your hands – not a problem. If you had bad experiences trying to budget in the past – don't let that hold you back. What you *do need to have* is a positive attitude and sense of purpose. A little common sense helps too, but the fact that you are even reading this guide suggests that you cleared this last hurdle.

This is not a "get rich quick" guide

This is a guide to financial *health*, not a guide to financial *wealth*. There's a difference. You will find plenty of books on the internet or in your local library or bookstore about how to become rich, but don't expect to find any secrets on that subject in the pages ahead. On the other hand, you may find it interesting that many of the people who *are* rich became that way through a keen understanding of how to budget their money and resources, which is what this book *is* all about.

Budgeting is not a novel idea

We hear about budgets all the time. Governments; corporations; churches; schools; non-profits; sports teams – they all have budgets. Budgeting might be done by an entire department (for example, the "financial planning department") or by a lone employee with a green eyeshade visor in a basement cubicle. Regardless of who is doing it, budgeting must get done. No group or entity could function well for very long without it.

You are no different; nor does it matter what your station in life is. You could be a billionaire with a flock of butlers, maids, gardeners, chefs, and chauffeurs; or, you could be a humble apartment renter who has to use a bus as your primary transportation. The principles don't change – only the individual circumstances.

Budgeting sounds like work

Budgeting requires discipline. Discipline, however, sounds like work. Raise your hand if you like to work. Very few of you flinched. Why? Because you're already working too much – whether it's holding down a couple of jobs; working too many hours in the one job you have; going to school and studying several hours after classes; looking for a job (which can be tremendously exhausting); or, perhaps the toughest scenario – you're a single parent caring for little ones at home all day.

If budgeting requires discipline, and discipline to you means work, then there is no point in sugarcoating it: budgeting *is* work. At this point, you may be thinking that the purchase of this guide was a waste of money, and ironically has contributed in a small way to your budgeting woes. Not so. Here's why. The rewards that result from budgeting are at least ten times greater than the efforts expended on budgeting.

The last sentence above bears repeating. *The rewards that result from budgeting are at least ten times greater than the efforts expended on budgeting.* To illustrate through a simple analogy, if I were to offer you $10 in exchange for $1, would that peak your interest? Of course it would. Budgeting has the same effect (or better). How did I arrive at a factor of ten? I'll show you through a very realistic example later on in this guide. Right now, the game plan is to warm you up to budgeting by getting you into the correct frame of mind. This is the hardest part of the process for most folks, because no matter how it's presented, budgeting will always sound like work.

What happens if I avoid budgeting?

The option is always there to skip the budgeting process altogether. After all, your time is valuable, budgeting is not exactly a mood enhancer, and you've managed to get by in life these many years without putting much effort or thought into budgeting. Moreover, your friends and family don't seem to dwell on the subject. Time to donate this book to Goodwill and turn the ball game on!

Really? Instead, maybe it's time to be honest with yourself. Look at your financial condition. Are you content? Given your track record, how much longer can you try to keep up with the Joneses? Every month you tell yourself things will improve, but they don't. In fact, they seem to be getting worse. To be sure, you can make an argument that it's really not your fault. After all, much of what we have to deal with in the financial world is out of our control – e.g., the economy, the price of gas, wages, interest rates, insurance, and taxes.

It's easy to lay the blame on outside forces and events. But that would be a big mistake, for the simple reason that it doesn't address your problem, which is that your financial health is in sad shape and deteriorating. The good news, however, is that because there is enough you *can* control, you can reverse the tide of bad fortune.

Procrastinating won't get the job done either. Suppose you convince yourself that you'll set aside time for budgeting when you have a quiet Saturday afternoon; or when you can take a precious day off from work; or when the kids are off at camp; or as soon as you upgrade your computer with the latest database software; or fill in your own excuse. The truth is (and you know it), procrastinating is nearly as bad as not budgeting at all. In fact, the psychological toll is worse, because the problem gnaws at you endlessly. Instead of facing the problem head on, you build additional walls of excuses to separate yourself from the problem. The end result is that your financial health never improves.

Forget the past

Forget the past. That's right; forget about whatever got you into your present financial mess. Forget about the poor decisions. Forget about the bad luck. Forget about the crazy purchases and foolish borrowing. Forget about the unsound investments. Forget about the bad timing; the unfair circumstances; the lapses in judgment; the silly missteps. Forget all that. It won't help you going forward, and will only divert precious energy that should be dedicated to improving your financial condition.   We can't go back in time. What was, was.

Wait, you say. Shouldn't we look to the past to make sure we don't repeat the same mistakes? That sounds logical. What I typically find, however, is that readers who take this approach stir up a nest of unpleasant memories, which only has a deflating effect. Moreover, because old habits are hard to break, people will unconsciously revert to these habits the more they dwell on them.   The best approach is to seal the old channels of thought and forge a fresh new path to financial health.

The past is beneficial in only one respect; certain expenses that you currently have and will have going forward are the result of decisions you made in your pre-budgeting life. Since you can't escape these expenses, you will need to review this part of your past as you budget for the future. For example, say you purchased a new car, and your payments are $300 a month over the next four years. While perhaps in hindsight you should have never bought the new car, that's not important for budgeting purposes. What *is* important is that, unless you plan on selling or trading the car, you will need to make monthly payments of $300 going forward. This will show up as an expense on your **Income Statement**, which we will discuss in detail in a later chapter.

Once you've stopped worrying about the past, and once you've convinced yourself that while budgeting may seem like work, it's worth your time and effort, you can start gearing up for the budgeting process.

Identify facts before choosing goals

Before we get into the mechanics of budgeting, let's pause to consider your mental approach to budgeting, and what your expectations should be. Like many people, you may be results-oriented by nature. That is, you set a goal (or result), and then move toward that goal, correcting your actions along the way whenever you veer off track. There are countless studies on human behavior that support this approach. Indeed, through self-programming, people will self-consciously make choices that steer them toward their ultimate goal. Or to put it differently, once the end is selected, the means will follow.

While I am a firm believer in the approach above, I would urge you to use great caution in how you implement it. Initially, any goal (i.e., result) you have in mind should be very generic. For example, it would be safe to say: "I would like to manage my budget so that by this time next year, I am in a position to take my family on a mini-vacation." What's wrong with setting more specific goals before budgeting? First, the goals may be entirely unrealistic, given the *facts* you have to deal with. Second, budgeting involves a holistic approach, where *after* gathering essential facts, you begin to make decisions about how to prioritize your spending. If you set a very specific goal in advance, the goal may need to be changed later on in the process. Thus, you will find that your actions initially track toward the "wrong" goal, which would not be encouraging.

Imagine, for example, that the CEO of a company announced that labor expenses were going to be cut by 50% next year. While that sounds like an ambitious goal, it could not be achieved unless there were some other means (e.g., automation) that supported a reduction in labor. But before that could be done, facts would have to be gathered to determine the expenses involved in setting up and running the machinery that would replace the workers. In other words, without an initial budget review, the announcement by the CEO could not take place.

Consider an example closer to home. Say your goal is to buy a brand new red jeep as a birthday gift to yourself. That's a great goal, and one possibly shared by thousands. However, is it a realistic goal? You wouldn't know until you gathered all the facts that provide the meat of your budget. Moreover, it may turn out that the only way you can purchase the jeep in such a short timeframe is to sacrifice some other need or desire you have. You always want to gather facts before you make specific goals or set priorities.

As I mentioned earlier, this guide will help lead you to financial health; financial *wealth*, on the other hand, is a topic for other guides. For example, I won't pretend to explain how you can secure a six-figure job when you're currently making $10 an hour. If I could do that, the red jeep you wanted wouldn't be an issue.

Finally, keep your expectations modest. As you begin practicing the art of budgeting, take strength from knowing that a consistent commitment to your budget plan will increasingly yield positive results. Much as a sick patient who faithfully takes antibiotics as prescribed improves his or her circumstances each day, the same occurs with budgeting. I call this the "ocean liner" effect. Turning an ocean liner 180 degrees isn't done in a few moments. It takes time and persistence. Or, if you like running, think of the process as a 5K race, and not a 100-meter sprint.

Chapter 2: The Art of Budgeting

In a nutshell, the desired budgeting process is this: First, you want to capture your entire financial condition. To do this, you complete a **Balance Sheet** that reflects your assets and liabilities, and an **Income Statement** that reflects your current income and expenses. Second, you prioritize your spending and consider savings opportunities. Third and lastly, you complete a **Budget Plan**, which shows what your expenses would ideally be after you have prioritized and considered savings opportunities.

Note that budgeting is as much an art as it is a science. The models and methods provided in this guide can be used by anyone, but individual circumstances and preferences differ so much that one person's budgeting end product is not the same as any other person's. However, there are some hard and fast rules to live by as you go through the budgeting process.

<u>Simple is good</u>

Simplicity is one of the most important keys to budgeting. This isn't to suggest that you need to make your life simpler. That may not be something you can do. But to budget effectively, you'll want to use methods that are simple, clear, straightforward and easy to replicate in the future when conditions change, or in the event several months pass between budgeting sessions. Simplicity is also crucial because you'll be making adjustments to your budget over time. If you have a sound structure in place, these adjustments will be easy to adopt.

Another reason for simplicity is a practical one – if the process is not simple, the chances of you staying on top of your budget will be slim. Let's face it. Most of us will take the time to learn something new if it benefits us in a big way. But we will drop it if the time spent on relearning it in the future is significant.

Simple is also best when you want to explain your budget to someone else, such as a family member. For some reason, a lot of people's eyes glaze over when numbers and math are discussed. This is a problem if the budget will affect others (e.g., a spouse) and you need their input in the budgeting process. Instead of being engaged, they will simply nod their heads in agreement (yet without understanding) or just throw their hands in the air and ask you to figure it out. In the worst case scenario, they will say that budgeting is fine as long as they can have [X]. Well, maybe [X] is the problem, and without a clear explanation of the budget, you'll find that you won't be able to make any progress.

Finally, the physical tools used for budgeting can be very simple. You don't need to purchase or know how to use programs such as Excel or Quicken. You don't need special accounting pads or financial workbooks. All you really need is a spiral bound notebook, a couple of pencils and a calculator. For under $10, you can be on your way to financial health.

Priorities matter

Before you complete your **Budget Plan**, you must prioritize. Sure, you may want to charter a yacht, take a trip to Rome, buy a sit-down lawn mower, get that leather purse you saw on sale, or snag seats in the fourth row at the 50-yard line. But the reality is that your expenditures are limited by your income stream (or at least they should be). Therefore, it is very important that you recognize the value of prioritizing during the budgeting process.

Prioritizing is critical because you may find that most of your expenses are fixed (i.e., cannot be changed); therefore, the amount of money you can spend with any discretion is quite limited. Prioritizing thus becomes the means by which you decide how to spend these discretionary funds. The idea, of course, is that your limited base of funds will grow as you make better financial decisions over time.

Be wary about taking prioritizing to an extreme. For instance, if you are an impulse buyer, don't try to convince yourself that it's okay to make a purchase because you suddenly decided it ranked high on your priority list. This would defeat the point of budgeting, as you need to take into account *all* of your financial needs, wants and options.

Will you spend money on a whim here and there? Certainly. You're not a robot.   But your **Budget Plan** should have money allocated for such expenditures. You might even add an expense item called "Impulse Purchases" to the **Budget Plan**, if that would put you at ease. (*I have added this item in the blank Budget Plan provided in Chapter 10.*)

Honesty is the best (and only) policy

This is your budget – nobody else's. You're not trying to compete with anyone, and you're not trying to convince the World how well you manage your money. To make it work, you have to be brutally honest with yourself about your spending habits and overall financial health. Otherwise, progress will be difficult or even nonexistent.

In a moment, I'll show you a sample **Balance Sheet** and **Income Statement**. You can complete your own using your particular circumstances. The **Balance Sheet** will provide you with a current snapshot of your assets and liabilities, and the **Income Statement** will show what your income and expenditures are on a monthly basis. As you fill in the figures, it is critical that you leave no stone unturned.

If, for example, you smoke 2 packs of cigarettes a day, are hooked on prescription drugs, or have a gambling habit that puts you in the red, the losses associated with these activities should be recorded in your budget. If you're making $300 a month selling stuffed animals at the flea market without telling the IRS, your budget will not judge you. You can and perhaps should change your poor habits and undesirable behavior going forward, but the budget itself should reflect reality.

Preparation makes all the difference

You can't just create a budget on the fly. There's a lot to capture. After all, most of what we do in life involves a financial outlay – whether it's eating, sleeping, traveling, or even breathing. Think about it. You could be using food stamps or taking advantage of a church or community food program, but that trip to McDonald's isn't free. The mattress you sleep on probably wasn't free. If you could avoid the cost of gasoline by simply bicycling to places, the bike itself, maintenance and a rain slicker would still set you back a few bucks. As for breathing, don't you pay taxes to support the government's efforts to reduce air pollution? The point is, most of the things we do cost money.

Before you start the budgeting process, I strongly suggest the following: For an entire calendar month, write down every single item you spent money on and the amounts that you spent. Will this represent exactly what you spend for an average month? No, because there are expenses you incur infrequently, seasonally, or on an annual basis. We will tackle these when you complete an **Income Statement**. Logging an entire month of expenditures, however, will give you a much truer sense of what you spend money on than if you merely sit down over a cup of coffee and try to figure it all out. I urge you to record your income in the same detailed manner.

Preparation also means that before you begin the budgeting process, you'll need to gather together anything that involves finances – e.g., checkbooks, credit card statements, pay stubs, auto insurance bills, sales contracts, utility statements, tax returns, life insurance plans, health insurance premiums and medical bills, IRA account and pension account statements, gift cards, copies of mortgages and mortgage notes, alimony agreements, leases, and even your piggybank. The more you get a handle on financial details, the more accurate your budgeting will be, and thus the more confident you'll be when you prepare a **Budget Plan**.

Budget adjustments improve financial health

When you have finally completed your **Balance Sheet** and **Income Statement**, you may not like what you see. Perhaps you thought you were in better financial shape. If that's the case, don't be discouraged. Certainly, sticking your head in the sand or lying in a fetal position won't solve anything.

As discussed earlier, adjustments can be made to improve your financial health, and these will be reflected in your **Budget Plan**. Some of these adjustments may be relatively easy; others may involve a more painful change in spending habits. If your situation is truly critical, even more drastic measures may need to be taken (e.g., taking on a second job, foreclosure, bankruptcy). We will review some of these unfortunate measures toward the end of the guide.

Chapter 3: The Balance Sheet

Your **Balance Sheet** records your assets and liabilities. *Assets* represent items for which a monetary *benefit* can be reasonably determined (e.g., your couch might be worth $200). *Liabilities* represent items for which a monetary *obligation* can be reasonably determined (e.g., $7,500 in principal left on a car loan).

Perhaps you are surprised to find a chapter devoted to the **Balance Sheet**. You may ask: Doesn't budgeting have to do with income and how you allocate income to expenses? It does indeed. The purpose of this guide, however, is to help you track and analyze those things that affect your financial health, and then to consider steps that might lead to improvement. Completing a **Balance Sheet** is an important part of the process. Some of your biggest expenses, for instance, are likely rooted in decisions you made that show up on your **Balance Sheet** (e.g., buying a house). Thus, how you manage your assets and liabilities going forward could have a great impact on your overall financial health. The alternative – applying financial band-aids – probably won't be sufficient.

After you have totaled your assets and liabilities, you can figure out your *Net Worth*, which is simply the sum of your assets minus the sum of your liabilities. For many people, this will be a negative number, which is a red flag, especially over the long term. Of course, it is true that you can't take your money to the grave with you. However, there are several reasons why you want to have a positive and growing net worth. For example –

✓ Social Security as we know it may not last too many more years, so to get stuck in a financial hole now is risky.

✓ You may wish to start a family, so it would be sensible to save now and be in a strong financial position for the day that happens.

✓ You have a short "bucket list" of things you would like to do, but you'll never be able to do any of them given your financial state.

✓ The stress of your current finances is negatively affecting other parts of your life, including relationships.

✓ You would like to be in a position to financially help family members, your church and your favorite charities.

✓ You wish to eventually leave something for your heirs.

Balance Sheet: Assets

The first of the two sections of the **Balance Sheet** reflects your assets. Assets are items that can generate cash flow, and include things you –

- own
- have a legal right to
- have a financial interest in

Do not consider liabilities as you identify your assets. For instance, suppose your house is worth $100,000, but you owe the bank $120,000. As an asset, enter $100,000, even though you clearly have no equity (i.e., net value) in the house. You would enter the $120,000 in the *Liabilities* section.

Below is an example of the *Assets* section of a **Balance Sheet**. The final chapter of this guide will contain a blank form for your use – or, as discussed earlier, you can create your own *Assets* section in a notebook (where you have plenty of room to make notes). Please note that if you have a family or significant other with whom you share assets, you'll want to complete a **Balance Sheet** that captures everyone's assets and liabilities.

Balance Sheet: Assets (example)

(1) Real Property (Values can be determined through a recent appraisal, your local property appraiser's office, or sites such as zillow.com.)

Home	$ 100,000
Second Property (e.g., condo as rental property)	80,000
Other	0

(2) Personal Property – Financial (most current values)

Cash on hand	$ 700
Savings deposits	2,000
Checking accounts	2,000
Certificates of deposit	4,000

Stocks, bonds and mutual funds (non-retirement)	10,000
Retirement accounts (e.g., 401K, IRA)	23,000
Security deposits (e.g., with landlord, utility companies)	0
Insurance payouts expected and due (e.g., life insurance)	0
Lawsuit or restitution payout expected and due	0
Commissions expected and due for past work	0
IOUs from friends or relatives	50
Tax return expected and due to you	0
Other	0

(3) Personal Property – Household Items, Transportation and Leisure. (Figures should represent estimates of what you could get if you sold these items.)

Automobile #1	$ 12,000
Automobile #2	0
Other vehicles (e.g., motorcycles, boats, bicycles, trailers)	4,000
Clothing and shoes	1,000
Furniture, lighting and paintings	3,000
Cookware, dishes and utensils	200
Appliances (e.g., refrigerator, stove, washing machine, toaster)	2,000
TVs	150
Electronics (e.g., computers, phones, stereos, game systems)	1,100
DVDs, CDs, tapes, books	175
Sports equip. (e.g., fishing pole, surfboard, guns, soccer ball)	600
Jewelry	400
Instruments (e.g., guitar)	80
Collectibles (e.g., stamps, rare coins, baseball cards)	100
Food (non-perishable)	30
Other	0

(4) Personal Property – Other

Animals (including pets)	$ 100
Tools and machinery	160
Lawn mower and gardening equipment	130
Stock in trade (i.e., inventory for work you may be performing)	0
Other	0

(5) Other

Inheritance or gift expected (monetary and property)	$ 0

Other	0

TOTAL ASSETS   **$ 246,975**

<u>Balance Sheet: Liabilities</u>

The second section of the **Balance Sheet** represents your liabilities, which are items that reflect –

- money, goods or services you owe to another person or entity

A word about debt: *Secured debt* represents a loan for which you signed an agreement listing property as security or collateral. A car loan would be a good example. But be careful. Debt you believe to be *unsecured* may not be. For instance, just because you acquired a card that appears to be your run-of-the-mill credit card doesn't mean that the debt isn't secured. Financial companies may not always be candid about the nature of the debt, so always ask whether debt is secured (and read the fine print) when signing up for a credit card.

Below is an example of the *Liabilities* section of a **Balance Sheet**. The final chapter of this guide will contain a blank form (or you can use a notebook for that purpose).

Balance Sheet: Liabilities (example)

(1) *Secured Debt and Liens* *(property as security or collateral)*

Mortgage – home	$ 120,000
Mortgage – second property (e.g., rental property)	95,000
Lease (lease amount left on property you rent)	0
Auto loan #1 (or lease) (amount remaining; includes interest)	13,000
Auto loan #2 (or Lease) (amount remaining; includes interest)	0
Other vehicle loans/leases (amounts remaining; includes int.)	0
Other secured debt (e.g., furniture, appliances, equipment)	800
Mechanic's liens (e.g., lien on house due to work on roof)	0
Other liens	0
Pawn shop and storage company loans	0
Other	0

(2) Unsecured Debt

Credit cards	$ 10,500
Payday loans	0
Medical bills	3,000
Debts you cosigned	0
Loans from relatives and friends	0
Loans on retirement funds	0
Student loans	2,000
Other unsecured loans/bills	0

(3) Other Obligations

Taxes owed to federal, state or local government	$ 0
Judgments, criminal restitution and traffic fines	50
Claims against you (amount likely to be owed)	0
Property settlement (e.g., with former spouse)	0
Amounts owed for services rendered (e.g., plumber, attorney)	100
Other obligations (that can be quantified)	0
Back rent	0
Other	0

TOTAL LIABILITIES   **$ 244,450**

NET WORTH

Total Assets less Total Liabilities = Net Worth
$ 246,975   - $ 244,450   = $ 2,525

In the example above, *Net Worth* is only $2,525. If the person for whom this example applied were a 40 year-old, the sad fact is that the net worth would be little more than his or her net worth as an 18 year-old – maybe even less if that 18 year-old lived at home, worked hard and saved.

If you look carefully at the figures above, some things should jump out at you. For instance, while the house, rental property and car are hefty assets, the amounts owed on them (i.e., liabilities) are even higher. Being "upside-down" is not uncommon, as housing prices have plummeted in many areas, and cars can lose up to 20% of their value the second they are driven off the lot.

Medical bills and credit card debt are also big items on the *Liabilities* side in the example above, which again, many people are struggling with in real life. (While student loans are not particularly high in the example, it is not unheard of for some young adults in real life to be on the hook for over $100,000.) Finally, the fact that there is only $23,000 saved for retirement is not encouraging. Unfortunately, this example is true to life for many folks. Naturally, very few people want to know that there is a good chance they will have to work into their 70s – but given the savings rate in the example above, this is what could happen.

Later on in this guide, we will discuss potential ways to help manage your assets and liabilities. Our focus now, however, will turn to income and expenses, which could be considered the heart of budgeting.

Chapter 4: The Income Statement

Your **Income Statement** records your income and expenses, which are shown on a monthly basis. *Income* can be from any source – not just wages. *Expenses* reflect the costs and taxes you incur, without regard for when you might actually pay for them. The difference between your income and your expenses is your *Net Income*, which you want to be a positive number.

As is the case with your **Balance Sheet**, if you have a family or significant other with whom you share finances, the **Income Statement** should reflect everyone's income and expenses, not just yours.

Income Statement: Monthly Income

Income may vary throughout the year. For example, say you expect to receive an income tax return of $600 every April. Your income would thus be shown as $50 ($600 ÷ 12 months), so as to spread the amount across 12 months. However, if the $600 tax return is a one-time event (i.e., it doesn't occur every year), then don't include it because you can't expect that income going forward.

You should spread out other irregular income the same way – but again, only if you can expect that income every year. For instance, you may work as a bartender every summer. Just add up all of the income from that job and divide by 12 to determine your monthly income.

Income Statement: Monthly Income (example)

Wages, bonuses and tips (job #1)	$ 5,417
Wages, bonuses and tips (job #2)	0
Pension income	0
Social Security	0
Food stamps	0
Unemployment compensation	0
Child support payments	0
Alimony	0

Welfare	0
Interest income	10
Annuities/fixed investment income	0
Stock dividends	80
Trust fund payouts	0
Tax return (typical refund)	67
Rental property income	1,000
Gifts (anticipated)	10
Payments from loans you have made to others	0
Garage sales (based on normal year)	0
Other	0

MONTHLY INCOME   **$ 6,584**

Income Statement: Monthly Expenses

Expenses, like income, can also vary throughout the year. Irregular expenses should be treated the same way you treated irregular income – by spreading the amounts equally over the months. For example, you may have your chimney cleaned once a year. If it costs $120, then your monthly expense would be $12 ($120 ÷ 12). Keep in mind that you would only record such expenses if you expected them to occur every year.

Note that *Expenses* represent costs, so be careful not to double count when you're considering your credit card expenses. For example, say you estimate your electricity bill to be $50/month, but you use a credit card to pay it. In that case, you would enter $50 on your **Income Statement** for electricity expense, but you would *not* include $50 as a credit card expense as well. Your credit card expense should *only* reflect the *finance charges* you incur each month based on your credit card balance. This is another reason why completing a **Balance Sheet** is so important – you can see your credit card balance in addition to the finance charges you are incurring on your **Income Statement**. Like a lot of folks, you may use credit cards to cover (or really avoid) your expenses, but if you don't pay the credit cards down, you'll eventually catch a financial flu.

Income Statement: Monthly Expenses (example)

(1) Taxes

Taxes on all sources of income (includes FICA, capital gains taxes)	$	1,354
Income tax return – amount you typically owe the government		0
Tax return preparation fees		0
Property taxes (if not included in mortgage payments)		160
Other		0

(2) Giving/Support

Tithing	$	100
Charities and other contributions		40
Gifts and cards		130
Support payments to relatives		0
Alimony and child support		0
Other		0

(3) Financial

Credit card finance charges	$	115
Pension/retirement		75
Education/Tuition savings program		0
Other		0

(4) Housing/Property Costs and Upkeep

Mortgage payments – home	$	600
Mortgage payments – second property		450
Rent		0
Condo/homeowners association fees		280
Utilities – trash pickup		40
Utilities – electricity		100
Utilities – gas		0
Utilities – water		40
Repairs (e.g., plumber, electrician, painter)		70
Maintenance (e.g., landscaping, pool cleaning, pest control)		100
House cleaning service		75
Home security		20
Tools		0
Other		0

(5) Insurance

Property (if not included in mortgage payments)	$	217
Renter's insurance		0
Health		300
Auto/Vehicles		120
Life		30
Other		0

(6) Home Life

Food & Drink	$	400
TV, computer, music, movies, internet, video games		200
Telephones		90
Furniture, paintings, ornaments		30
Newspapers, magazines and books (non-school)		25
Household goods (e.g., toiletries, detergent, cookware, dishes)		15
Cosmetics		15
Clothing and shoes		70
Diapers		0
Parties		0
Other		0

(7) Vehicles

Loan installment payments	$	333
Lease payments		0
Gasoline and tolls		180
Maintenance and repair		40
Registration and licensing fees		35
Public transportation		0
Other		0

(8) Outside Interests/Entertainment

School and recreational classes (including books/materials)	$	50
Vacations (e.g., travel, hotels, cruises, camping)		200
Memberships (e.g., civic clubs, fitness)		50
Visual Arts (e.g., movies, musicals, plays)		20
Events (e.g., sports, concerts)		17
Restaurants and bars		100
Camps (for kids)		0

Other entertainment (e.g., theme parks)		0
Other		0

(9) Personal Services

Medical and dental (includes meds) – out of pocket costs	$	15
Personal care (salons, haircuts, massage, nails)		30
Personal Services (e.g., lawyer, therapist)		100
Professional laundry		10
Other		0

(10) Other Expenses

Other Loan installment payments (e.g., furniture, medical)	$	40
Garnishment		0
Pets (e.g., food, cleaning, boarding, medical)		100
Day care		0
Collectibles		0
Cigarettes/Cigars		150
Sports equipment		0
Jewelry		10
Union dues		0
Other		0

MONTHLY EXPENSES   **$ 6,741**

MONTHLY NET INCOME

Monthly Income less Monthly Expenses = Monthly Net Income
$ 6,584   - $ 6,741   =   ($ 157)

In the example above, *Monthly Net Income* was negative. It was negative even though by most people's standards, *Monthly Income* (at $6,584) was very respectable. This leads to a couple of questions.   First, how did this person come up with the $157 to cover the difference? The answer is through incurring more debt, and this often means incurring more credit card debt at a high interest rate – which over time is a real budget killer. Just look at your credit card statements and see if the balance due is growing over time. Each successive **Balance Sheet** will also tell you what liabilities are growing over time.

The second question you may have is what can be done to make the *Monthly Net Income* positive, so that extra funds can be used to pay off debt, save, or achieve other goals you have in mind? The next three chapters are dedicated to answering this question. In Chapter 5, we will consider spending priorities, and in Chapters 6 and 7, we will look at potential savings opportunities.

Chapter 5: Setting Priorities

In Chapter 4, you were shown an example of an **Income Statement**. Revisit the *Monthly Expenses* section of that **Income Statement** and consider this basic question: Are the dollar amounts for those items necessary? More specifically, are the amounts:

(1) "Fixed"? That is, does the budgeter lack any ability to change them (e.g., income taxes, auto loan payments)?

(2) "Needs"? That is, does the budgeter *believe* that the amount being spent on each item is necessary? Or, does some portion of an amount merely represent a "want"? For example, you need food, but you don't *need* to eat filet mignon every night. So part of the *Food & Drink* expenses (i.e., a certain percentage) could really just represent a "want."

My hunch is that you know the answers to these questions as they pertain to your *own* financial situation and individual preferences. In all likelihood, there are several items for which the amounts could be reduced – *just by prioritizing*.

To illustrate how prioritizing works, we will reprint the *Monthly Expenses* section of the example in Chapter 4, but exclude any items that showed an expense of $0. We will also add two columns. In the first new column, we will estimate the percentage spent that is either (1) "fixed" or (2) a "need." In the second new column, we will multiply current expenses by those percentages.

Thus, to take our *Food & Drink* example, suppose the budgeter believed that of the $400 currently expensed, only 80% of it represented a "fixed" amount or a "need." The second column would thus show $320. In other words, current expenses are being reduced by "wants" to arrive at amounts that only reflect "fixed" amounts and "needs."

Certainly, you can get more sophisticated and rank items, or label items as "fixed," "strong need," "need," "strong want," or "want" – and then decide what amounts should be included (and thus excluded). This would be more accurate.

However, I would encourage you to use the simple approach I have outlined above – at least the first time you work through your own figures.

Finally, <u>do not be tempted to *increase* any of the amounts during this budgeting stage</u>. For instance, suppose you believe that the amount you currently tithe is not only a 100% "need," but that the figure should be doubled. Do not revise this number up. It's best to hold off on increasing any amounts until you have completed the prioritizing stage and considered *all* savings opportunities (as discussed in Chapters 6 and 7). Then, as you create your **Budget Plan** (in Chapter 8), you'll be able to allocate any newfound funds to items that you deem to be the most important to you.

Let's now consider our *Monthly Expenses* example to see how setting priorities can make a difference.

WANTS   NEEDS   FIXED

Income Statement: Monthly Expenses (example)

	Current Amounts	% "Fixed" or "Needs"	Revised Amounts
(1) Taxes			
Taxes on all sources of income (includes FICA, capital gains taxes)	$ 1,354	100 %	$ 1,354
Property taxes (if not included in mortgage payments)	160	100%	160
(2) Giving/Support			
Tithing	$ 100	100%	$ 100
Charities and other contributions	40	50%	20
Gifts and cards	130	50%	65
(3) Financial			
Credit card finance charges	$ 115	100%	$ 115
Pension/retirement	75	100%	75
(4) Housing/Property Costs and Upkeep			
Mortgage payments – home	$ 600	100%	$ 600
Mortgage payments – second property	450	100%	450
Condo/homeowners association fees	280	100%	280
Utilities – trash pickup	40	100%	40

Utilities – electricity	100	80%	80
Utilities – water	40	80%	32
Repairs (e.g., plumber, electrician, painter)	70	100%	70
Maintenance (e.g., landscaping, pool cleaning, pest control)	100	100%	100
House cleaning service	75	80%	60
Home security	20	100%	20

(5) Insurance

Property (if not included in mortgage)	$ 217	100%	$ 217
Health	300	80%	240
Auto/Vehicles	120	100%	120
Life	30	50%	15

(6) Home Life

Food & Drink	$ 400	80%	$ 320
TV, computer, music, movies, internet, video games	200	75%	150
Telephones	90	80%	72
Furniture, paintings, ornaments	30	40%	12
Newspapers, magazines and books (non-school)	25	80%	20
Household goods (e.g., toiletries, detergent, cookware, dishes)	15	100%	15
Cosmetics	15	80%	12
Clothing and shoes	70	60%	42

(7) Vehicles

Loan installment payments	$ 333	100%	$ 333
Gasoline and tolls	180	100%	180
Maintenance and repair	40	100%	40
Registration and licensing fees	35	100%	35

(8) Outside Interests/Entertainment

School and recreational classes (including books/materials)	$ 50	100%	$ 50
Vacations (e.g., travel, hotels, cruises, camping)	200	50%	100
Memberships (e.g., civic clubs, fitness)	50	100%	50
Visual Arts (e.g., movies, musicals, plays)	20	100%	20

Events (e.g., sports, concerts)	17	80%	14
Restaurants and bars	100	70%	70
(9) Personal Services			
Medical and dental (includes meds) – out of pocket costs	$ 15	100%	$ 15
Personal care (e.g., salons, haircuts, massage)	30	80%	24
Personal Services (e.g., lawyer, therapist)	100	75%	75
Professional laundry	10	80%	8
(10) Other Expenses			
Other Loan installment payments	$ 40	100%	$ 40
Pets	100	80%	80
Cigarettes/Cigars	150	50%	75
Jewelry	10	0%	0

MONTHLY EXPENSES	**$ 6,741**	**$ 6,065**

By removing "wants" from *Monthly Expenses*, the budgeter has trimmed an incredible $676 ($6,741 less $6,065). Now, instead of a negative *Monthly Net Income* of $157, the budgeter has a potential positive *Monthly Net Income* of $519 (-$157 plus $676)!

Keep in mind that prioritizing is unique to each person. Thus, when it comes to deciding what amount comprises a "need" and what amount comprises a "want," use your own judgment. In the example above, for instance, the budgeter felt that 50% of his or her prior cigarette use represented a "need." To many people, smoking is not a "need." But then again, those same people aren't seeing it from the perspective of the budgeter. Perhaps next year, the budgeter could reduce the dollar amount for cigarettes to zero.

By prioritizing, you are taking a huge step toward creating a **Budget Plan**. The other big step involves looking at potential savings opportunities, which is the subject of our next chapter.

Chapter 6: Savings Opportunities

Even after making adjustments through prioritizing, you might not like what you see. Moreover, you're pretty sure a boost in income isn't on the near horizon. Relax. Breathe. Without all of this newfound knowledge, your financial health could very well get worse. Reality isn't always pleasant, but it can be a great motivator. Also keep in mind what I said earlier about the "ocean liner" effect. Turning an ocean liner 180 degrees isn't done in a few moments. It takes time and persistence.

Fortunately, there is often "low hanging fruit," which over time could add significant savings. Many of these savings ideas can be found through your own internet research, and I strongly encourage you to investigate. For example, just enter the words "savings tips" in an internet search engine; you could literally spend hours writing these tips down.

In the pages below, you may find several ideas that improve your financial picture.

AUTOMOBILES

- **Check your tire pressure every month**. You can find a gauge for under $10. According to the U.S. Department of Energy, under-inflated tires can lower gas mileage by 0.3 percent for every 1 psi drop. So, for example, if your tires are supposed to be 35 psi, but you've been driving them at 30 psi, that could mean an extra $4 a month in gas costs. There are also costs associated with the additional wear and tear.
- **Use regular gasoline**. According to the California Energy Commission, if you own a modern car, a higher-grade gasoline won't help you much (unless your owner's manual requires it). Switching from premium to regular leads to huge savings.
- **Go easy on the pedal**. According to the Federal Trade Commission, driving at 75 mph, rather than 65 mph, can increase fuel consumption by an additional 25%. With current gas prices, that can add up in a hurry.

ATMs

- **Avoid withdrawing small amounts**. Perhaps you think you can keep spending under control by withdrawing $20 here, $30 there. Think again. First, the $3 withdrawal fees will add up over time. Second, you'll lose track of how much you've been withdrawing. You would actually spend less if you withdrew a larger amount (e.g., $500) and paced yourself. Finally, with all the news reports about ATM security risks, you should give yourself some peace of mind and withdraw less frequently.

BARTERING

- **Cut out the middleman**. You can reduce the costs of selling one item and then buying another by good old-fashioned trading. For example, if your enthusiasm for boating has declined, and you are now into muscle cars, check out craigslist.com for bartering opportunities (under the "for sale" section).

COFFEE

- **Go easy on the Frappuccinos®**. Can't shake that coffee buzz? Love the vibe of your local coffee shop? Who can blame you? The problem is that you may be dropping $80 a month on this habit. You can cut back by making coffee at work or home, and stock up on milk and honey to take the edge off. If you love hanging out at cafes, try to limit your visits to twice a week.

CONSIGNMENT STORES

- **Find bargains on clothes, furniture, paintings and knick knacks**. I bet you've driven by a consignment store countless times and never stopped in. Well, stop in. You'd be amazed at the good stuff people are trying to unload. And you can always negotiate because it's up to the consignors (not the stores) as to what they're willing to accept. On the lower end, thrift stores can also have some great bargains.

ENERGY

- **Turn the thermostat down to 60° at night during the cold season**. This might seem extreme, but you can do this and be comfortable if you wear socks, gloves and a wool hat to bed. (Most of our internal heat gets lost through our extremities.) Close the vents in unused rooms while you're at it.

- **Install a programmable thermostat**. According to the U.S. Environmental Protection Agency, you can save up to $180 a year by installing a programmable thermostat (which might cost $50).
- **Weather stripping will save you a bundle**. Does it seem like your heating system goes on every 5 minutes during those cold days, or that your air-conditioning comes on just as frequently on the hot ones? Blame those mini-drafts. You can put a stop to them by sealing doors and windows. For seepage around non-movable objects, you may be able to apply caulking. Also, don't forget that drapes and blinds are great insulators.
- **Set your water heating temperature at 120°**. According to the U.S. Department of Energy, you can save up to 5% of water heating costs for each 10° decrease in water temperature.
- **Replace furnace filters**. When filters get clogged, they can put a major drag on your system, which leads to higher energy costs. Filters are inexpensive, so there's no excuse for overlooking this easy cost-saver.
- **Use fans**. They are much cheaper to run than air conditioning.
- **Stuff that freezer**. A full freezer is more efficient, as there is less room for hot air to circulate. If you don't have food to fill it with, anything will do (e.g., milk jugs full of water).
- **Switch to fluorescent**. Florescent light bulbs use less electricity and last longer. One word of caution: they do give some people headaches.
- **Invest in a clothesline**. Save on those clothes dryer costs and invest in a clothesline for under $20. At least use it for the big stuff like towels and sheets. An inexpensive clothes rack serves the same purpose.
- **Turn off lights you aren't using**. This is a no-brainer.

EXTENDED WARRANTIES
- **These are usually not recommended**. Nothing more than a high-priced insurance policy, an extended warranty might not even cover the problem, and repairs will often be cheaper than the policy. If you lack such

confidence in the purchase you're considering, maybe you should rethink the purchase.

FINANCIAL

- **Do your own taxes**. If you've been having your tax returns prepared by someone else, but your financial life has not become more complex, then consider doing your own taxes. Tax forms and publications for most folks don't change much from year to year. And surely you received a copy of your returns to use as an example. In fact, doing taxes is really part of the budgeting process, as you can see firsthand how income and expenses are affected by tax rules.

- **Negotiate down your credit card rates**. Of course, this is hard to do if your credit isn't great. However, you can research other cards on the market (e.g., cardtrak.com, indexcreditcards.com), and see if you're eligible for one with a reasonable rate. If you are, you can use this as leverage to reduce rates on current cards. Be careful about those "0% interest for a year" offers. If you can't pay down your balance, you could end up being stuck with even higher rates. Finally, always ask about having your annual card fee waived.

- **Save on checking fees**. Use automatic bill payments if possible. Not only will this reduce the amount of checks you write; it will also save on postage and keep you from forgetting to pay.

GARAGE SALES

- **Check them out regularly**. You don't need to waste gas and time traveling for miles trying to hit every garage sale. Most weekends, you'll see a garage sale sign within a 2-mile radius of home. Just do a drive-by. If it looks promising, stop. Sure, the likelihood is small that you'll find something you need, but if you do, you can be assured that it'll have a small price tag. Another benefit is that you get to meet folks in your community in a relaxed setting.

GIFTS and CARDS

- **Buy gift cards on-line**. Save up to 30 percent by buying gift cards on-line – for example, check out plasticjungle.com, giftcardrescue.com, cardpool.com and swapagift.com. While these sites don't list every store or movie theatre, they're definitely worth a couple clicks of the mouse. For restaurant gift certificates, try restaurant.com.

- **Your Sunday paper has a second purpose (or really third, if you count news and coupons)**. Use the comics section of the Sunday paper as gift-wrapping paper. If that doesn't seem presentable enough, then reuse wrapping paper, bows and ribbons you've saved from prior celebrations.

- **Agree to forego gift-giving**. Propose to family and friends new approaches to gift-giving. For example, instead of a gift, make a promise that you'll do something for the other person (e.g., join them in a hike, mow their lawn, babysit, etc.). Or, agree to set a limit on the amount that can be spent per gift (e.g., $20). You can also get creative. For instance, instead of a gift, send a card with a thoughtful poem. This will be much appreciated.

GROCERIES and HOUSEHOLD PRODUCTS

- **Buy in bulk**. If you have the storage space, buy what you use a lot of in large quantities. (This even applies to clothes, such as socks and underwear.) The cost savings can be huge, and should easily defray any big box store membership dues you may need to pay (e.g., Costco, Sam's Club). Fewer shopping visits could also lead to savings in gas costs.

- **Focus your coupon-hunting**. Who has the luxury of spending all day looking for coupons? Limit your search to a few sources, such as store websites, the Sunday paper and sites such as coupons.com, couponmom.com and smartsource.com. Note that some stores accept competitors' coupons, so be sure to ask.

- **Forget the canned beans**. Buy bags of beans and cook a big pot of them all at once. Then freeze individual portions. Do the same thing for rice. This should last you several meals. Similarly, save big on money and time by buying large family packets of meat, which you can weigh, cut, wrap and freeze.

- **Garden your way to savings**. Growing a garden can not only save you money; it can also calm your mind and decrease stress.

- **Cut your juice costs in half**. Dilute your juice so it's half juice and half water. Just like switching from whole milk to 1% milk, it won't take you long to get used to it. After a while, 100% juice will seem incredibly rich.

- **Save on laundry detergent**. Like juice, you don't need to use 100% of the recommended amount. Who says you have to pour to the level indicated on the cap? Try cutting the suggested amount in half and see if your clothes still smell fresh. Chances are they will.

- **Use store brands**. Don't let fancy branding relieve you of your hard-earned money. If the quality of the end product is good, who cares about the packaging? And sometimes no packaging is best – for example, a head of lettuce and simple homemade dressing can be much cheaper than a pre-washed salad kit.

- **Discount stores are worth a visit**. Discount stores obviously carry low-priced goods. However, don't assume that you're getting great value for every item. Also, you'll need to resist the urge to buy stuff you haven't budgeted.

GYM MEMBERSHIPS

- **Stay committed**. We all know the story. You join a gym on January 2, pay for a membership that lasts 6 months or a year, and then stop going a month later. So why sign up in the first place? Well, the problem doesn't seem to be one of finances, but one of commitment. $35 a month is not a huge outlay for getting healthy, which can result in other cost savings (e.g., medical costs).

HAIR and NAILS

- **Gentlemen, don't be sucked in by the $25 (and up) cuts**. Sure, the fancy hair salons appear more upscale, and you may get your hair shampooed. But the mom and pop barber shops can do as good a job for half the price.

- **Ladies, keep those nails short and natural**. Cut down on those manicure visits, and watch your budget improve dramatically. Besides, a nice polish will be quite attractive on its own.

INSURANCE

- **Consider bundling**. Some insurance outfits will give you a discount if you use them for your different insurance needs (e.g., house *and* car).

- **Raise your deductibles**. Reducing your health insurance premiums in exchange for higher deductibles may be very worthwhile. Use the last year or two as a predictor. Did you come close to bumping up against your deductibles? If no, and if your health is stable, you could save quite a bit by reducing those premiums. Consider higher deductibles for auto insurance as well. Finally, reconsider what you're paying for life insurance. Death visits us all at some point, but don't let that morbid thought drive you into making irrational payments.

- **Shop around and compare**. Insure.com allows you to compare rates in different insurance categories – e.g., house, auto, health, and life. Other helpful sites include insweb.com and freeinsuranceadvice.com. Sure, switching involves paperwork; but the savings can be substantial.

- **Learn about discount opportunities**. Call your insurance companies and ask about ways to reduce your rates. For instance, some health insurers will give a discount if you complete a health and wellness program. Some auto insurers will reduce your rate if you have safe driving habits or use a security system. Also, your car insurance rate should decline as your car ages, due to depreciation. If not, threaten to switch to another auto insurer.

- **Avoid installments**. If you can afford it, pay insurance for a full 6 months or a year instead of through monthly installment payments. For auto insurance, this could mean a savings of $5 a month.

LIBRARIES

- **Who can argue with free**? Libraries have books, CDs, DVDs and magazines. If your computer is out of service or you can't afford one – head to the library. Need a tutor? You may find one at the library. Want your kids to get excited about reading? The library may have a reading program. These services may not truly be free in that your tax dollars support the library, but that's even more of a reason to take advantage of this great community resource.

LUNCH

- **Brown bag your lunch**. How many times have you gone to lunch with friends or co-workers and told yourself you wouldn't spend more than $5, but end up spending twice that? You can easily save $60 a month by bringing your lunch to work instead, whether it's in a trusty lunch pail or in plastic containers – and that's still allowing yourself one day out to splurge. Plus, you can still join your friends on the other days by eating first and just ordering a water as your friends spend their hard-earned money.

LAWN MOWING

- **Mow your own lawn**. Yeah, this is a pain, especially on those scorching hot days. But it could save you over $50 a month, and provide you with the exercise you've been neglecting. If you need a mental or physical break now and then, contract with a lawn-mowing service or neighborhood kid – just not every week.

MEDICAL

- **Negotiate those bills**. Providers have discretion to reduce bills, so it doesn't hurt to seek a discount. This is especially true if you're having a lot of services done. If you can't afford a bill, ask to get on a payment plan.

- **Urgent care may be a good option**. Urgent care facilities are often a better option than emergency rooms, which can have long wait times. Such facilities can also be much cheaper if you have a high deductible or co-pay.

- **Samples, samples, samples**. If you need to take medication, always ask your doctor for samples. Also ask about medication discount cards and specials. Doctors are very busy and don't always know what the latest specials are, but they can refer you to staff who will have that knowledge. But they might not do that if you don't ask. Finally, ask your doctor if you can cut your pills in half, as this may provide considerable savings through higher dosage purchases.

- **Save on pet meds**. If you can get medication for your pets on-line or through a drugstore or big box retailer, this may be a much cheaper route than through your vet.

MISCELLANEOUS

- **Use low print settings**. As you well know, ink cartridges aren't cheap. So unless that document is real important, use the lowest print setting possible.

- **Unsubscribe**. If you're no longer using that news publication or dating website you subscribed to, it's probably time to cancel. The same goes for magazines you no longer have the time or desire to read.

- **Coupon websites do help**. Sites such as shopathome.com, couponchief.com, mycoupons.com retailmenot.com provide some great savings. Remember, don't just buy something because you found a coupon. It should be part of your budget in the first place. The same can be said for phone and TV service websites such as billshrink.com, or video game websites such as gamestop.com.

- **Buy used sports equipment**. Trying a new sport? Don't spend hundreds of dollars just to see if you'll like it. Drop by used sports equipment stores such as Play it Again Sports® for good deals.

- **Wash Fido yourself**. By the time you take your pet down to have it professionally groomed, you could have done it yourself. Hey, do you want to save money or not?

- **Have the cleaners come less often**. If you hate doing major cleaning, at least save yourself money by reducing the frequency of cleaning service visits. Do light cleaning yourself and have the professionals come *every other* month.

- **Compare rates before shipping**. If you ship often or have a large item to ship, it pays to compare rates. Uship.com is one site that'll get you that information – with no limitations on size or destination.

PARKING IN THE CITY

- **Avoid expensive parking garages**. Parking garages, while convenient, can be very expensive. I was in Ft. Lauderdale for business one time and parked in a garage, only to find out later that the rate was $8 an hour. You can also avoid meters if you park several blocks from your destination. A little exercise will do you good and let you use the money on something truly meaningful.

PERSONAL CARE

- **Check out technical and beauty schools**. These schools, which are training tomorrow's estheticians and hygienists, provide low-cost massages, facials, pedicures, manicures and teeth cleaning.

PHONES

- **Drop the landline**. If possible, make your cell phone your home phone.

- **Consider prepaid calling plans**. Review the last few months of your phone usage. If the minutes and texting were light, then an inexpensive prepaid calling plan may be just the ticket. Most of the carriers have them.

- **Get that activation fee waived**. If opening a new line or even upgrading or extending an existing contract, your carrier may try to hit you with an activation fee. Threaten to cancel if that's their practice.

- **Avoid or minimize cancellation fees**. Try to argue your way out of a cancellation fee. Your carrier may be receptive. If that doesn't work, consider websites such as celltradeusa.com, which will match you up with someone who wants a shorter or less expensive plan.

- **Need to sell your phone?** You can sell your cell phone (and Apple® products) through gazelle.com.

RESTAURANTS

- **Split the entrée**. Entrée servings are usually large. So if there are two of you eating out, save money by getting an appetizer and splitting an entrée. Loading up on free bread or chips before you decide on the main meal can also save you a bunch.

- **Check for early-bird specials**. Retirees in the Sunbelt have been taking advantage of early-bird specials for years. What's also good about these is that they often coincide with happy hour specials, where drinks are sold at a reduced price and appetizers are sometimes free.

- **Look for** discounts. You can often find on-line savings for restaurant chains (e.g., eatdrinkdeals.com), and there are many restaurants where kids eat free (e.g., mykidseatfree.com). If you consider yourself a senior citizen, don't hesitate to ask about senior discounts.

- **Eat before you eat**. That's right! Have a snack or eat a light meal at home before you go out to eat, so you don't "buy" the menu.

SOUP

- **Soup is good for the frugal soul**. Soups can be very cheap to make – just throw in whatever you have lying around in your fridge or pantry. It's your soup. Chicken broth as a base is inexpensive if you find water to be too spartan for your taste. Crock pots and slow cookers are great if you want to come home to a ready-made meal.

TRAVEL and VACATIONING

- **Ask for the corporate rate**. If you stop in a hotel without a reservation, quietly ask for the corporate rate. Chances are the clerk won't even ask for employment evidence.

- **Don't rent your car at the airport**. Avoid all of the extra fees and rent from an agency that's offsite.

- **Watch those airline baggage fees**. While you may think you're booking the cheapest flight, the deal may not look so hot once you factor in the baggage and seat selection fees. Learn about add-on costs for each airline before you make travel plans. Also keep in mind that flights are often cheaper on Tuesdays, Wednesdays and Saturdays, which are days when business travelers and vacationers are least likely to fly.

- **Consider AAA**. If you take a lot of road trips, you get the benefit of roadside assistance, along with discounts on auto repairs, hotels and rentals.

- **Include a trip to an outlet mall in your travels**. Go to outletbound.com to find out where all the outlet malls are.

TV and MOVIES

- **Downgrade your provider contract**. Do you really need hundreds of channels? Are you seeking couch potato elite status? Seriously, you can cut back service and combine with internet services for less than what you may be currently paying.

- **Movies on the cheap**. New video-streaming services are popping up all the time. Many of these deals won't hit you in the pocketbook if you cancel later on. If you need your theatre fix once in a while, go to a matinee – it's much cheaper than the evening shows and you won't have to fight the crowds.

WATER

- **Skip the bottles**. The quality of bottled water may not be any better than what comes out of your faucet. If you're still concerned about the health risks, you can save a boatload of money by purchasing filters – either the kind that attach to your faucet or the ones that come with a pitcher.

- **Take shorter showers**. The sensible thing would be to buy a shower head that reduces water flow. But then a lot of people will just take longer showers. If you need water gushing at you, stick with the flow you have, but cut your showers down to 5 minutes. Reward yourself with a long shower or nice bath once a week.

- **Water your lawn in the early morning hours**. Don't become a victim of mid-day evaporation.

- **Turn off water while brushing your teeth or scrubbing dishes**. Enough said.

Chapter 7: Savings Adjustments

After you've considered potential savings opportunities, you can once again adjust the *Monthly Expenses* section of your **Income Statement**. This time, you will start with the figures you arrived at after you made your priority adjustments.

By way of example, we will take the numbers from the "Revised Amounts" column of the *Monthly Expenses* sheet in Chapter 5 and enter them in the "Post-Priorities" column below. Then, we will subtract savings opportunities to calculate "New Revised Amounts."

Income Statement: Monthly Expenses (example)

	Post - Priorities	Savings Potential	New Revised Amounts
(1) Taxes			
Taxes on all sources of income (includes FICA, capital gains taxes)	$ 1,354	$ 0	$ 1,354
Property taxes (if not included in mortgage payments)	160	0	160
(2) Giving/Support			
Tithing	$ 100	$ 0	$ 100
Charities and other contributions	20	0	20
Gifts and cards	65	15	50
(3) Financial			
Credit card finance charges	$ 115	10	$ 105
Pension/retirement	75	0	75
(4) Housing/Property Costs and Upkeep			
Mortgage payments – home	$ 600	0	$ 600
Mortgage payments – second property	450	0	450
Condo/homeowners association fees	280	0	280
Utilities – trash pickup	40	0	40
Utilities – electricity	80	10	70
Utilities – water	32	3	29
Repairs (e.g., plumber, electrician, painter)	70	10	60
Maintenance (e.g., landscaping, pool	100	20	80

cleaning, pest control)			
House cleaning service	60	20	40
Home security	20	0	20

(5) Insurance

Property (if not included in mortgage)	$ 217	0	$ 217
Health	240	40	200
Auto/Vehicles	120	10	110
Life	15	5	10

(6) Home Life

Food & Drink	$ 320	30	$ 290
TV, computer, music, movies, internet, video games	150	20	130
Telephones	72	0	72
Furniture, paintings, ornaments	12	0	12
Newspapers, magazines and books (non-school)	20	5	15
Household goods (e.g., toiletries, detergent, cookware, dishes)	15	3	12
Cosmetics	12	0	12
Clothing and shoes	42	2	40

(7) Vehicles

Loan installment payments	$ 333	0	$ 333
Gasoline and tolls	180	10	170
Maintenance and repair	40	0	40
Registration and licensing fees	35	0	35

(8) Outside Interests/Entertainment

School and recreational classes (including books/materials)	$ 50	0	$ 50
Vacations (e.g., travel, hotels, cruises, camping)	100	40	60
Memberships (e.g., civic clubs, fitness)	50	0	50
Visual Arts (e.g., movies, musicals, plays)	20	0	20
Events (e.g., sports, concerts)	14	0	14
Restaurants and bars	70	10	60

(9) Personal Services

Medical and dental (includes meds) – out of	$ 15	3	$ 12

pocket costs			
Personal care (e.g., salons, haircuts, massage)	24	4	20
Personal Services (e.g., lawyer, therapist)	75	0	75
Professional laundry	8	0	8
(10) Other Expenses			
Other Loan installment payments	$ 40	0	$ 40
Pets	80	10	70
Cigarettes/Cigars	75	0	75
Jewelry	0	0	0

MONTHLY EXPENSES   **$ 6,065**   **- $ 280**   **$ 5,785**

By including savings opportunities, the budgeter has reduced expenses by an additional $280. This brings *Monthly Net Income* to a positive $799 ($519 plus $280).

Recall that in Chapter 1, I claimed that *the rewards that result from budgeting are at least ten times greater than the efforts expended on budgeting*. With the example we've been using, you can see how this is possible. After including priorities and savings opportunities, the budgeter reduced monthly expenses from $6,741 to $5,785, which is nearly $1,000. If the budgeter valued his or her free time at $20 an hour, and spent 5 hours on the budgeting process, that would amount to $100, or only one-tenth of the amount that could be saved.

In the next chapter, we will determine how these revised *Monthly Net Income* dollars should be spent as we prepare a **Budget Plan**.

Chapter 8: The Budget Plan

The stage is now set to create a **Budget Plan**. Essentially, *Monthly Net Income* (which is hopefully positive at this point) is allocated to the areas you deem most important. This sounds easy, but it really takes careful thought and discipline. Many readers will see all this newfound "free money" and be tempted to splurge on things that make them happy. It's only human nature. However, since this guide is about improving financial health, you wouldn't let yourself down by doing that, would you?

From the example we have been using, *Monthly Net Income* is now $799. How do we allocate this? Well, for starters, the budgeter should recognize that credit card finance charges, which were originally eating up $115 a month, were not providing anything of value. Also, from the **Balance Sheet**'s *Liabilities*, we can see that outstanding credit card debt is $10,500 – not a tiny sum. Taking aggressive steps to pay this down makes sense.

Another area that may be suitable for an increase is retirement. The current contribution of $75 a month, while better than nothing, will not be adequate for retirement purposes, even if expensed over many years.

Growing personal savings should also be a consideration. From the **Balance Sheet**'s *Assets*, we can see that the amounts for cash on hand, savings deposits and checking accounts total $4,700. This may seem like a lot, but for many people it represents only a couple of months of living expenses. It might be wise to boost this figure to provide a financial cushion in the event of a lay-off or emergency.

How you allocate your revised *Monthly Net Income* is of course up to you. Keep in mind, however, that instant gratification through financial means should not interfere with your goal of achieving financial health.

Finally, note that the **Budget Plan** should show *all Monthly Expense* items, not just the ones that are being expensed.

BUDGET PLAN (example): *$799 to be allocated*

(1) Taxes	New Revised Amounts	$799 to be Allocated	YOUR BUDGET
Taxes on all sources of income (includes FICA, capital gains taxes)	$ 1,354	$ 0	$ 1,354
Income tax return – amount you typically owe the government	0	0	0
Tax return preparation fees	0	0	0
Property taxes (if not included in mortgage payments)	160	0	160
Other	0	0	0

(2) Giving/Support

Tithing	$ 100	$ 100	$ 200
Charities and other contributions	20	10	30
Gifts and cards	50	0	50
Support payments to relatives	0	0	0
Alimony and child support	0	0	0
Other	0	0	0

(3) Financial

Credit card finance charges	$ 105	$ 300	$ 405
Pension/retirement	75	125	200
Education/Tuition savings program	0	0	0
Other	0	0	0

(4) Housing/Property Costs and Upkeep

Mortgage payments – home	$ 600	$ 0	$ 600
Mortgage payments – second property	450	0	450
Rent	0	0	0
Condo/homeowners association fees	280	0	280
Utilities – trash pickup	40	0	40
Utilities – electricity	70	0	70
Utilities – gas	0	0	0
Utilities – water	29	0	29
Repairs (e.g., plumber, electrician, painter)	60	0	60
Maintenance (e.g., landscaping, pool cleaning, pest control)	80	0	80

House cleaning service	40	0	40
Home security	20	0	20
Tools	0	0	0
Other	0	0	0

(5) Insurance

Property (if not included in mortgage)	$ 217	$ 0	$ 217
Renter's insurance	0	0	0
Health	200	0	200
Auto/Vehicles	110	0	110
Life	10	0	10
Other	0	0	0

(6) Home Life

Food & Drink	$ 290	$ 40	$ 330
TV, computer, music, movies, internet, video games	130	0	130
Telephones	72	0	72
Furniture, paintings, ornaments	12	0	12
Newspapers, magazines and books (non-school)	15	0	15
Household goods (e.g., toiletries, detergent, cookware, dishes)	12	0	12
Cosmetics	12	0	12
Clothing and shoes	40	0	40
Diapers	0	0	0
Parties	0	0	0
Other	0	0	0

(7) Vehicles

Loan installment payments	$ 333	$ 0	$ 333
Lease payments	0	0	0
Gasoline and tolls	170	0	170
Maintenance and repair	40	0	40
Registration and licensing fees	35	0	35
Public transportation	0	0	0
Other	0	0	0

(8) Outside Interests/Entertainment

School and recreational classes (including books/materials)	$ 50	$ 0	$ 50
Vacations (e.g., travel, hotels, cruises, camping)	60	20	80
Memberships (e.g., civic clubs, fitness)	50	0	50
Visual Arts (e.g., movies, musicals, plays)	20	0	20
Events (e.g., sports, concerts)	14	0	14
Restaurants and bars	60	15	75
Camps (for kids)	0	0	0
Other entertainment (e.g., theme parks)	0	0	0
Other	0	0	0

(9) Personal Services

Medical and dental (includes meds) – out of pocket costs	$ 12	$ 0	$ 12
Personal care (e.g., salons, haircuts, massage)	20	0	20
Personal Services (e.g., lawyer, therapist)	75	0	75
Professional laundry	8	0	8
Other	0	0	0

(10) Other Expenses

Other Loan installment payments	$ 40	$ 0	$ 40
Garnishment	0	0	0
Pets	70	0	70
Daycare	0	0	0
Collectibles	0	0	0
Cigarettes/Cigars	75	0	75
Sports equipment	0	0	0
Jewelry	0	0	0
Union dues	0	0	0
Other	0	0	0

BUDGET $ 5,785 $ 610 $ 6,395

In this example, only $610 of the $799 to be allocated is budgeted for *Monthly Expenses*. How will the remaining $189 be allocated? It will go to increasing the budgeter's **Balance Sheet** assets, such as cash on hand, savings deposits or checking accounts. By increasing these assets (at least until the next budget review), the budgeter will create a stronger financial safety net in the event unforeseen problems occur (e.g., lay-off, medical emergency).

In Chapter 10, you will be able to work through the entire budgeting process to arrive at your own **Budget Plan**. I highly recommend that you do this at least twice a year and whenever your financial condition or individual preferences change appreciably.

Before we unleash you to create your own budget, we will consider some tips and strategies that you may find useful in your pursuit of financial health.

Chapter 9: Tips and Strategies

It's one thing to create a budget. It's another thing to follow the budget and maintain the proper financial mindset. In this next-to-last chapter, we'll consider strategies that will help you do just that. We'll also look at options that may be available to you in the event you cannot achieve financial health through budgeting.

Savings Tips

✓ **Just say no (or maybe).** Get in the habit of saying *no*. When you see those cool shoes on sale at 40% off, be strong. Just say *no* (unless new shoes truly are included in your budget). Get it in your head that the word "sale" is not the same as the word "buy." The same applies for coupons. If saying *no* is that difficult, say *maybe*, but give yourself at least three days to mull it over. Hopefully your buying fever will subside. Finally, always ask yourself if something is a "need" in the first place.

✓ **Ask for a discount**. The worst that can happen is that the sales clerk says *no*, and you'll be surprised how many times you'll hear the word *yes*. Of course, how you pitch it helps. For example, you might start the conversation by saying "I like that chair, but I only planned on spending [X] amount. Do you know if it'll be going on sale anytime soon?" If you use a little diplomacy, and don't blurt out to the entire store that you're looking for a discount, you just might get a reduced price.

✓ **Buy off-season**. So you want to buy a boat? Don't buy at the beginning of the boating season. Christmas gifts? If you really want to save, wait until after the holidays when stores dump their inventory. The point is that timing is key, which means you need to exercise patience. So even if your budget suddenly looks rosier and you have funds for a major purchase, don't become an easy target for a sales rep. The same applies to traveling – which tends to be much cheaper off-season.

✓ **Use savings and not your credit card to pay for vacations**. This really applies to any purchase, not just vacations. There is nothing wrong with using a credit card for a transaction, as long as you can quickly pay the amount off in full without incurring a finance charge. This is important. In the *Monthly Expenses* example we've been using in this guide, current credit card finance charges are $115 a month. Why? Because the budgeter was not disciplined. Those finance charges represent real money that could be used for something of true value to the budgeter.

✓ **Never shop on an empty stomach**. The hungrier you are, the more food you will buy, including goodies that normally wouldn't make the list.

✓ **If you have kids, make them earn their allowance**. By doing this, for example, you could greatly reduce professional house cleaning costs and expenses related to landscaping or pool cleaning services.

✓ **Do free (or inexpensive) stuff**. Some people feel like the only way they can avoid spending money is by staying at home. That's not true. Take a frisbee to the park. Go for a bike ride. Attend a high school play or sporting event. Take up gardening. Go for a hike. Volunteer. Head to the library. Do some local sight-seeing. Visit friends. If you can keep things simple and avoid over-scheduling yourself (and your family), you'll probably see some savings.

✓ **Do your shopping homework**. Search for reviews of stores and products through google.com. Go on-line to find savings articles (e.g., stretcher.com).

✓ **Learn to be a handyman**. Why pay others to do what you can not only do yourself, but also take pride in? There are plenty of do-it-yourself resources, both in print and on-line (e.g., ehow.com, bejane.com, doityourself.com, homedepot.com, walmart.com).

✓ **Be wary of "free trials" and on-line subscriptions**. Watch out for those inviting websites that entice you to sign up with a credit card, but don't give you an exit plan. You've seen them. These are sites that don't have an icon for cancelling, and while they list a "customer care" number, you end up being put on hold forever or are asked to leave a message. Always look for on-line reviews of these outfits or check the Better Business Bureau for any complaints before signing up.

✓ **Pay off debt with the highest interest rate first**. This will usually be your credit card debt. For other loans, be sure to consider tax deductions. For example, if you can deduct for a house loan with a 6% interest rate but not for a vehicle loan with a 5% rate, then the vehicle loan probably has the higher effective rate.

✓ **Give your time to charity**. Instead of donating money, consider donating your time, which you might find more personally satisfying.

✓ **Renegotiate contracts.** From auto insurance to phone plans to credit cards, it could be a worthy endeavor. Your negotiating leverage will be stronger if you can get pre-approval for competitor deals.

✓ **Improve your credit**. Pay down your balances and make payments on time. Reduce the number of credit cards down to one or two, but do this very gradually, as length of credit history and available credit could affect your credit score. A reduction in cards will mean less risk of theft and better management of your expenses; plus, the likelihood of you forgetting to pay your bills on time will fall. You can get a free credit report annually through a credit bureau. Try transunion.com, equifax.com or experian.com.

✓ **Take advantage of friends and neighbors**. Don't rush out to buy a tool that you'll only use one time, when you can borrow one from next door. Hit up friends for movies and CDs.

✓ **Don't buy lottery tickets**. The odds are horrible.

Asset Management

Unless you have deep pockets, your biggest purchases are typically made through financing, which translates to large monthly expenses over several years. Prime examples are real estate and automobiles. Try to think of these major purchases as investments, for which you would like a return, whether monetary or otherwise. These items show up as *Assets* on your **Balance Sheet**. We've already discussed in Chapter 3 how many folks are "upside down" in terms of the value of these assets and their corresponding debt.

In the case of houses, many people struggle with the decision whether to rent or buy. We won't cover that topic in this guide. However, if you happen to be one of these people, it obviously makes sense to consider many factors, including taxes, maintenance, insurance, length of stay, rental costs, equity gains, and salability. There are also non-financial considerations, such as the intrinsic benefits that come with ownership. Websites such as smartmoney.com and ourfamilyplace.com provide a starting point for considering the pros and cons of renting versus buying.

If you already own your home, look into refinancing your loan. If you can knock a few percentage points off, this could be a big saver. Just check the fees and terms very carefully. If you're thinking of tapping your home's equity for money, consider the risk involved, particularly given today's economic uncertainties. You can't reduce debt with debt. However, this strategy shouldn't be completely ruled out if you can take advantage of the tax deductions, and if the debt will be used to pay down high interest loans.

Exercise similar caution for automobile purchases. New cars and trucks depreciate very quickly post-purchase and have higher insurance rates. Also, you'll be stuck with big monthly expenses for years. So, while you might grumble over a $500 repair bill on an older model vehicle that's been paid off, that $500 may amount to less than two months of payments on a new vehicle. If you do decide to buy a new vehicle, scale the model to what you can afford. Remember, who cares about the Joneses?

Leasing a car may not make sense financially, unless you plan to keep the vehicle for just a few years. Check out bankrate.com, smartmoney.com, leaseguide.com and federalreserve.gov/pubs/leasing for the pros and cons of leasing versus buying.

If you decide to buy instead of lease, keep in mind that with shorter term loans, you'll pay less interest. When the loan rate is higher than the inflation rate, you're losing money on the difference. Thus, a shorter loan period will be beneficial (and allow you to build equity quicker). Of course, the downside is that your monthly expenses will be larger. Finally, it's a good idea to get pre-approved financing before you even set foot on a car lot, so you can avoid high rates and finance charges.

Other Considerations

This guide would not be complete without at least touching on those unfortunate scenarios where budgeting is not enough – that is, where financial circumstances are so dire that drastic steps need to be taken.

If you're buried in debt and high interest rates, and your income is not sufficient to keep your head above water, and there is no hope for financial health, then filing for bankruptcy may be an option. There should be no shame in taking this route. Famous and accomplished people have done it, including Henry Ford, Walt Disney, P.T. Barnum and Donald Trump. Millions of others do it annually. You're no different. If you feel you need to consider bankruptcy, I advise finding a reputable bankruptcy attorney in town and schedule a free or low-cost confidential consultation.

Debt consolidation loans are of course another option, but these can be quite dangerous. Many people have been harmed by such loans, due to fees and other conditions in the fine print. Moreover, unsecured debt can all of a sudden become secured debt. If you're considering consolidation, be sure to research the credit counseling service through the Better Business Bureau or your state consumer protection agency.

Finally, if you own a house, but are months behind in payments, it's best to proactively try to work things out through your loan servicer. Loan modification rules have more teeth than they used to, so borrowers may be able to benefit from lower interest rates, extended loan periods and reductions in principal. Short sales, waivers of deficiencies and deeds in lieu of foreclosure are potential options in the event of a foreclosure lawsuit. If you're facing such a scenario, do not hesitate to seek legal advice.

It is my hope that you never face such challenges, and that your road leads instead to financial health. The budgeting exercise in Chapter 10 should help guide you along that road.

Chapter 10: Your Budget

This final chapter is devoted strictly to you and your budget. As a refresher, the steps are as follows:

1. Complete your **Balance Sheet**, which includes the values of your *Assets* and *Liabilities*.
2. Complete your **Income Statement**, which includes *Monthly Income* and *Monthly Expenses*.
3. Revise your *Monthly Expenses* by setting priorities.
4. Revise your *Monthly Expenses* a second time by including savings opportunities.
5. Create your **Budget Plan** by allocating net income.

While templates for these steps are provided below, feel free to work through the budgeting process using a separate notebook.   I wish you much success on your journey to financial health!

STEP 1 – BALANCE SHEET

Balance Sheet: Assets

(1) Real Property (Values can be determined through a recent appraisal, your local property appraiser's office, or sites such as zillow.com.)

Home	$
Second Property (e.g., condo as rental property)	
Other	

(2) Personal Property – Financial (most current values)

Cash on hand	
Savings deposits	
Checking accounts	
Certificates of deposit	
Stocks, bonds and mutual funds (non-retirement)	
Retirement Accounts (e.g., 401K, IRA)	
Security deposits (e.g., with landlord, utility companies)	
Insurance payouts expected and due (e.g., life insurance)	

Lawsuit or restitution payout expected and due	
Commissions expected and due for past work	
IOUs from friends or relatives	
Tax return expected and due to you	
Other	

(3) Personal Property – Household Items, Transportation and Leisure. *(Figures should represent estimates of what you could get if you sold these items.)*

Automobile #1	
Automobile #2	
Other vehicles (e.g., motorcycles, boats, bicycles, trailers)	
Clothing and shoes	
Furniture, lighting and paintings	
Cookware, dishes and utensils	
Appliances (e.g., refrigerator, stove, washing machine, toaster)	
TVs	
Electronics (e.g., computers, phones, stereos, game systems)	
DVDs, CDs, tapes, books	
Sports equip. (e.g., fishing pole, surfboard, guns, soccer ball)	
Jewelry	
Instruments (e.g., guitar)	
Collectibles (e.g., stamps, rare coins, baseball cards)	
Food (non-perishable)	
Other	

(4) Personal Property – Other

Animals (including pets)	
Tools and machinery	
Lawn mower and gardening equipment	
Stock in trade (i.e., inventory for work you may be performing)	
Other	

(5) Other

Inheritance or gift expected (monetary and property)	
Other	

TOTAL ASSETS $ _____

Balance Sheet: Liabilities

(1) *Secured Debt and Liens* (property as security or collateral)	Amount Outstanding
Mortgage – home	$
Mortgage – second property (e.g., rental property)	
Lease (lease amount left on property you rent)	
Auto loan #1 (or lease) (amount remaining; includes interest)	
Auto loan #2 (or Lease) (amount remaining; includes interest)	
Other vehicle loans/leases (amounts remaining; includes int.)	
Other secured debt (e.g., furniture, appliances, equipment)	
Mechanic's liens (e.g., lien on house due to work on roof)	
Other liens	
Pawn shop and storage company loans	
Other	

(2) *Unsecured Debt*	
Credit cards	
Payday loans	
Medical bills	
Debts you cosigned	
Loans from relatives and friends	
Loans on retirement funds	
Student loans	
Other unsecured loans/bills	

(3) *Other Obligations*	
Taxes owed to federal, state or local government	
Judgments, criminal restitution and traffic fines	
Claims against you (amount likely to be owed)	
Property settlement (e.g., with former spouse)	
Amounts owed for services rendered (e.g., plumber, attorney)	
Other obligations (that can be quantified)	
Back rent	
Other	

TOTAL LIABILITIES $ _____

NET WORTH

Total Assets	less	Total Liabilities	=	Net Worth
$_____	-	$_____	=	$_____

STEP 2 – INCOME STATEMENT

Income Statement: Monthly Income

Wages, bonuses and tips (job #1)	$
Wages, bonuses and tips (job #2)	
Pension income	
Social Security	
Food stamps	
Unemployment compensation	
Child support payments	
Alimony	
Welfare	
Interest income	
Annuities/fixed investment income	
Stock dividends	
Trust fund payouts	
Tax return (typical refund)	
Rental property income	
Gifts (anticipated)	
Payments from loans you have made to others	
Garage sales (based on normal year)	
Other	

MONTHLY INCOME $ _____

Income Statement: Monthly Expenses

(1) Taxes

Taxes on all sources of income (includes FICA, capital gains taxes)	$
Income tax return – amount you typically owe the government	
Tax return preparation fees	
Property taxes (if not included in mortgage payments)	
Other	

(2) Giving/Support

Tithing	

Charities and other contributions	
Gifts and cards	
Support payments to relatives	
Alimony and child support	
Other	

(3) Financial

Credit card finance charges	
Pension/retirement	
Education/Tuition savings program	
Other	

(4) Housing/Property Costs and Upkeep

Mortgage payments – home	
Mortgage payments – second property	
Rent	
Condo/homeowners association fees	
Utilities – trash pickup	
Utilities – electricity	
Utilities – gas	
Utilities – water	
Repairs (e.g., plumber, electrician, painter)	
Maintenance (e.g., landscaping, pool cleaning, pest control)	
House cleaning service	
Home security	
Tools	
Other	

(5) Insurance

Property (if not included in mortgage payments)	
Renter's insurance	
Health	
Auto/Vehicles	
Life	
Other	

(6) Home Life

Food & Drink	
TV, computer, music, movies, internet, video games	

Telephones	
Furniture, paintings, ornaments	
Newspapers, magazines and books (non-school)	
Household goods (e.g., toiletries, detergent, cookware, dishes)	
Cosmetics	
Clothing and shoes	
Diapers	
Parties	
Other	

(7) Vehicles

Loan installment payments	
Lease payments	
Gasoline and tolls	
Maintenance and repair	
Registration and licensing fees	
Public transportation	
Other	

(8) Outside Interests/Entertainment

School and recreational classes (including books/materials)	
Vacations (e.g., travel, hotels, cruises, camping)	
Memberships (e.g., civic clubs, fitness)	
Visual Arts (e.g., movies, musicals, plays)	
Events (e.g., sports, concerts)	
Restaurants and bars	
Camps (for kids)	
Other entertainment (e.g., theme parks)	
Other	

(9) Personal Services

Medical and dental (includes meds) – out of pocket costs	
Personal care (salons, haircuts, massage, nails)	
Personal Services (e.g., lawyer, therapist)	
Professional laundry	
Other	

(10) Other Expenses

Other Loan installment payments (e.g., furniture, medical)	

Pets (e.g., food, cleaning, boarding, medical)	
Day care	
Collectibles	
Cigarettes/Cigars	
Garnishment	
Sports equipment	
Jewelry	
Union dues	
Other	

MONTHLY EXPENSES $ _____

NET INCOME

Monthly Income less Monthly Expenses = Monthly Net Income
$ _____   - $ _____   = $ _____

Note: Monthly expenses above become the Current Amounts in Column 1 of STEP 3 below (Setting Priorities).

STEP 3 – SETTING PRIORITIES

Income Statement: Monthly Expenses

WANTS   NEEDS   FIXED

(1) Taxes	Current Amounts	% "Fixed" or "Needs"	Revised Amounts
Taxes on all sources of income (includes FICA, capital gains taxes)	$	%	$
Income tax return – amount you typically owe the government			
Tax return preparation fees			
Property taxes (if not included in mortgage payments)			
Other			
(2) Giving/Support			
Tithing			
Charities and other contributions			
Gifts and cards			
Support payments to relatives			
Alimony and child support			
Other			
(3) Financial			
Credit card finance charges			
Pension/retirement			
Education/Tuition savings program			
Other			
(4) Housing/Property Costs and Upkeep			
Mortgage payments – home			
Mortgage payments – second property			
Rent			
Condo/homeowners association fees			
Utilities – trash pickup			
Utilities – electricity			
Utilities – gas			
Utilities – water			
Repairs (e.g., plumber, electrician, painter)			
Maintenance (e.g., landscaping, pool			

cleaning, pest control)			
House cleaning service			
Home security			
Tools			
Other			

(5) Insurance

Property (if not included in mortgage)			
Renter's insurance			
Health			
Auto/Vehicles			
Life			
Other			

(6) Home Life

Food & Drink			
TV, computer, music, movies, internet, video games			
Telephones			
Furniture, paintings, ornaments			
Newspapers, magazines and books (non-school)			
Household goods (e.g., toiletries, detergent, cookware, dishes)			
Cosmetics			
Clothing and shoes			
Diapers			
Parties			
Other			

(7) Vehicles

Loan installment payments			
Lease payments			
Gasoline and tolls			
Maintenance and repair			
Registration and licensing fees			
Public transportation			
Other			

(8) Outside Interests/Entertainment

School and recreational classes (including books/materials)			
Vacations (e.g., travel, hotels, cruises, camping)			
Memberships (e.g., civic clubs, fitness)			
Visual Arts (e.g., movies, musicals, plays)			
Events (e.g., sports, concerts)			
Restaurants and bars			
Camps (for kids)			
Other entertainment (e.g., theme parks)			
Other			

(9) Personal Services

Medical and dental (includes meds) – out of pocket costs			
Personal care (e.g., salons, haircuts, massage)			
Personal Services (e.g., lawyer, therapist)			
Professional laundry			
Other			

(10) Other Expenses

Other Loan installment payments			
Pets (e.g., food, cleaning, boarding, medical)			
Day care			
Collectibles			
Cigarettes/Cigars			
Garnishment			
Sports equipment			
Jewelry			
Union dues			
Other			

MONTHLY EXPENSES $ _____ $ _____

Note: Revised Amounts in Column 3 above become the Revised Amounts in Column 1 of STEP 4 below (Savings Opportunities).

STEP 4 – SAVINGS OPPORTUNITIES

Income Statement: Monthly Expenses

(1) Taxes	Revised Amounts	Savings Potential	New Revised Amounts
Taxes on all sources of income (includes FICA, capital gains taxes)	$	$	$
Income tax return – amount you typically owe the government			
Tax return preparation fees			
Property taxes (if not included in mortgage payments)			
Other			
(2) Giving/Support			
Tithing			
Charities and other contributions			
Gifts and cards			
Support payments to relatives			
Alimony and child support			
Other			
(3) Financial			
Credit card finance charges			
Pension/retirement			
Education/Tuition savings program			
Other			
(4) Housing/Property Costs and Upkeep			
Mortgage payments – home			
Mortgage payments – second property			
Rent			
Condo/homeowners association fees			
Utilities – trash pickup			
Utilities – electricity			
Utilities – gas			
Utilities – water			
Repairs (e.g., plumber, electrician, painter)			

Maintenance (e.g., landscaping, pool cleaning, pest control)			
House cleaning service			
Home security			
Tools			
Other			

(5) Insurance

Property (if not included in mortgage)			
Renter's insurance			
Health			
Auto/Vehicles			
Life			
Other			

(6) Home Life

Food & Drink			
TV, computer, music, movies, internet, video games			
Telephones			
Furniture, paintings, ornaments			
Newspapers, magazines and books (non-school)			
Household goods (e.g., toiletries, detergent, cookware, dishes)			
Cosmetics			
Clothing and shoes			
Diapers			
Parties			
Other			

(7) Vehicles

Loan installment payments			
Lease payments			
Gasoline and tolls			
Maintenance and repair			
Registration and licensing fees			
Public transportation			

Other			

(8) Outside Interests/Entertainment

School and recreational classes (including books/materials)			
Vacations (e.g., travel, hotels, cruises, camping)			
Memberships (e.g., civic clubs, fitness)			
Visual Arts (e.g., movies, musicals, plays)			
Events (e.g., sports, concerts)			
Restaurants and bars			
Camps (for kids)			
Other entertainment (e.g., theme parks)			
Other			

(9) Personal Services

Medical and dental (includes meds) – out of pocket costs			
Personal care (e.g., salons, haircuts, massage)			
Personal Services (e.g., lawyer, therapist)			
Professional laundry			
Other			

(10) Other Expenses

Other Loan installment payments			
Pets (e.g., food, cleaning, boarding, medical)			
Day care			
Collectibles			
Cigarettes/Cigars			
Garnishment			
Sports equipment			
Jewelry			
Union dues			
Other			

MONTHLY EXPENSES $ _____ - $ _____ $ _____

MONTHLY NET INCOME (revised after setting priorities and including savings opportunities)

Monthly Income less Monthly Expenses = Monthly Net Income
$ _____   - $ _____   = $ _____

Note:

- Monthly Net Income = Amount to be Allocated in your **Budget Plan** (STEP 5)

- New Revised Amounts in Column 3 above become the New Revised Amounts in Column 1 of the **Budget Plan** (STEP 5).

STEP 5 – BUDGET PLAN

BUDGET PLAN: *$_____ to be allocated (= Monthly Net Income in STEP 4 above)*

(1) Taxes	New Revised Amounts	$_____ to be Allocated	YOUR BUDGET
Taxes on all sources of income (includes FICA, capital gains taxes)	$	$	$
Income tax return – amount you typically owe the government			
Tax return preparation fees			
Property taxes (if not included in mortgage payments)			
Other			
(2) Giving/Support			
Tithing			
Charities and other contributions			
Gifts and cards			
Support payments to relatives			
Alimony and child support			
Other			
(3) Financial			
Credit card finance charges			
Pension/retirement			
Education/Tuition savings program			
Other			
(4) Housing/Property Costs and Upkeep			
Mortgage payments – home			
Mortgage payments – second property			
Rent			
Condo/homeowners association fees			
Utilities – trash pickup			
Utilities – electricity			
Utilities – gas			
Utilities – water			

Repairs (e.g., plumber, electrician, painter)			
Maintenance (e.g., landscaping, pool cleaning, pest control)			
House cleaning service			
Home security			
Tools			
Other			

(5) Insurance

Property (if not included in mortgage)			
Renter's insurance			
Health			
Auto/Vehicles			
Life			
Other			

(6) Home Life

Food & Drink			
TV, computer, music, movies, internet, video games			
Telephones			
Furniture, paintings, ornaments			
Newspapers, magazines and books (non-school)			
Household goods (e.g., toiletries, detergent, cookware, dishes)			
Cosmetics			
Clothing and shoes			
Diapers			
Parties			
Other			

(7) Vehicles

Loan installment payments			
Lease payments			
Gasoline and tolls			
Maintenance and repair			
Registration and licensing fees			

Public transportation			
Other			

(8) Outside Interests/Entertainment

School and recreational classes (including books/materials)			
Vacations (e.g., travel, hotels, cruises, camping)			
Memberships (e.g., civic clubs, fitness)			
Visual Arts (e.g., movies, musicals, plays)			
Events (e.g., sports, concerts)			
Restaurants and bars			
Camps (for kids)			
Other entertainment (e.g., theme parks)			
Other			

(9) Personal Services

Medical and dental (includes meds) – out of pocket costs			
Personal care (e.g., salons, haircuts, massage)			
Personal Services (e.g., lawyer, therapist)			
Professional laundry			
Other			

(10) Other Expenses

Other Loan installment payments			
Garnishment			
Pets			
Daycare			
Collectibles			
Cigarettes/Cigars			
Sports equipment			
Jewelry			
Union dues			
Impulse purchases			
Other			

$_____ $_____ $_____

Remaining amount (if any) to be allocated: $ _____ . To which **Balance Sheet** Asset(s) will these additional funds be allocated? _____ _____.

*** CONGRATULATIONS. YOU HAVE COMPLETED YOUR BUDGET ***